Robots

Melissa Stewart

NATIONAL GEOGRAPHIC

Washington, D.C.

Published by Collins
An imprint of HarperCollins*Publishers*
The News Building
1 London Bridge Street
London
SE1 9GF

Browse the complete Collins catalogue at
www.collins.co.uk

In association with National Geographic Partners, LLC

NATIONAL GEOGRAPHIC and the Yellow Border Design
are trademarks of the National Geographic Society, used
under license.

Second edition 2018
First published 2014

Copyright ©2014 National Geographic Partners, LLC. All
Rights Reserved.

Copyright ©2018 British English edition National
Geographic Partners, LLC. All Rights Reserved.

ISBN 978-0-00-831739-3

10 9 8 7 6 5 4 3

All rights reserved. No part of this publication may be
reproduced, stored in a retrieval system, or transmitted,
in any form or by any means, electronic, mechanical,
photocopying, recording or otherwise without the prior
permission in writing of the publisher and copyright
owners.

The contents of this publication are believed correct
at the time of printing. Nevertheless the publisher can
accept no responsibility for errors or omissions, changes
in the detail given or for any expense or loss thereby
caused.

HarperCollins does not warrant that any website
mentioned in this title will be provided uninterrupted,
that any website will be error free, that defects will be
corrected, or that the website or the server that makes
it available are free of viruses or bugs. For full terms and
conditions please refer to the site terms provided on the
website.

A catalogue record for this book is available from the
British Library

Printed and bound in China by RR Donnelley APS

If you would like to comment on any aspect of this book,
please contact us at the above address or online.
natgeokidsbooks.co.uk
cseducation@harpercollins.co.uk

Paper from responsible sources

Since 1888, the National Geographic Society has
funded more than 12,000 research, exploration, and
preservation projects around the world. The Society
receives funds from National Geographic Partners,
LLC, funded in part by your purchase. A portion of the
proceeds from this book supports this vital work. To learn
more, visit http://natgeo.com/info.

Photo Credits
Abbreviations: GI = Getty Images; SS = SuperStock
Cover, Ed Alcock for Aldebaran Robotics; 1, Akihiro I/GI;
4 and 5, 6–7, George Steinmetz/National Geographic
Creative; 8 (UP), Ralph Crane/Time Life Pictures/GI;
8 (LOLE), SS RM/GI; 8 (LORT), SS; 9 (UPLE), Bettmann/
Corbis; 9 (UPRT), GI; 9 (LOLE), AFP/Newscom; 9, NASA; 11,
SS; 12 (UP), Leonhard Foeger/Reuters; 12 (LOLE), Matthew
Walker; 12 (LORT), Peter Menzel/Science Photo Library;
13 (UP), provided by RIKEN-TRI Collaboration Center for
Human-Interactive Robot Research; 13 (CTR LE), Sheng Li/
Reuters/Corbis; 13 (CTR RT), Katsumi Kasahara/Gamma-
Rapho/GI; 13 (LO), SSPL/GI; 14, Ed Darack/Science Faction/
Corbis; 15 (UP), Alain Le Bot/Photononstop/Corbis; 15 (LO),
AFP PHOTO/Yoshikazu Tsunoyoshikazu Tsuno/AFP/GI/
Newscom; 16 (LE), George Steinmetz/National Geographic
Creative; 16 (RT), BSIP/UIG/GI; 17 (LE), Robert Clark/
National Geographic Creative; 17 (RT), Jonathan Searle/
Reuters/Corbis; 18, DARPA/Science Photo
Library; 18 (INSET), Willee Cole/Shutterstock; 19, Amanda
Loman/Virginia Tech College of Engineering; 19 (INSET),
AdStock RF/Shutterstock; 20, cellistka/Shutterstock;
21, Yoshikazu Tsuno/AFP/GI/Newscom; 22–23,
ricardoazoury/E+/GI; 24, courtesy Defense Advanced
Research Projects Agency (DARPA); 25, NASA/Carnegie
Mellon University/Science Photo Library; 26, Stephen
Roberts Photography/Alamy; 27, yne News/WENN/
Newscom; 28, courtesy Rob Felt/Georgia Institute of
Technology; 29, Kim Kyung-Hoon/Reuters/Corbis; 30,
Science Photo Library Rf/GI; 31, Yoshikazu Tsuno/AFP/
GI/GI; 32, AP Images/Vincent Thian; 33, AP Images/
Koji Sasahara; 34, Peter Menzel/Science Source; 35
(1–4), Peter Menzel/Science Source; 36 (LE), Albert L.
Ortega/WireImage/GI; 36 (RT), Richard Nowitz/National
Geographic Creative; 37 (UP), Blue Sky Studios/20th
Century Fox/Bureau L.A. Collection/Corbis; 37 (LOLE),
Digital Domain/20th Century Fox/Bureau L.A. Collection/
Corbis; 37 (LORT), John M. Heller/GI; 38, NASA/JPL/Science
Photo Library; 39, 40–41, NASA; 40 (INSET), NASA; 41
(INSET), NASA; 42, Photo by Adriana Groisman, courtesy of
FIRST®; 43 (UPLE), Photo by Argenis Apolinario, courtesy
of FIRST®; 43 (UPRT, LOLE, LORT), Photo by Adriana
Groisman, courtesy of FIRST®; 44–45, Pedro Ladeira/AFP/
GI; 46 (UPRT), Robert Clark/National Geographic Creative;
46 (CTR LE), George Steinmetz/National Geographic
Creative; 46 (CTR RT), DARPA/Science Photo Library; 46
(LOLE), George Steinmetz/National Geographic Creative;
46 (LORT), NASA; 47 (UPLE), AP Images/Koji Sasahara; 47
(UPRT), NASA/SS; 47 (CTR LE), Science Photo Library RF/GI;
47 (CTR RT), Yoshikazu Tsuno/AFP/GI/Newscom; 47 (LOLE),
Peter Menzel/Science Source

Table of Contents

What's a Robot?

What do you think of when you hear the word ROBOT? A blinking, walking, robo-talking metal person? Some robots really do look like people, but most don't.

A robot copies human motion while playing table tennis.

Robots come in almost every shape, size and colour you can think of. They can look like fish or flies, lobsters or spiders. Some look like nothing else you've ever seen.

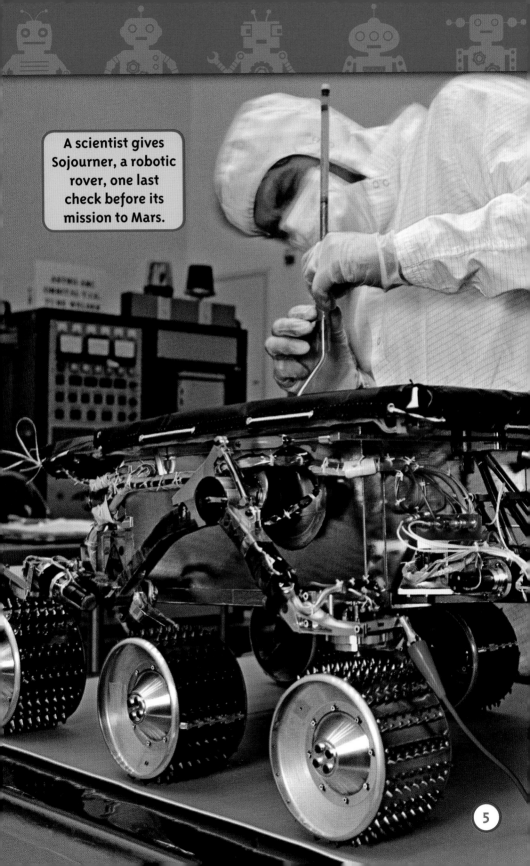

A scientist gives Sojourner, a robotic rover, one last check before its mission to Mars.

A robot, or bot, is a machine that has movable parts and can make decisions. People design it to do a job by itself.

How is a robot like a person? It collects information from its surroundings.

A robot in Japan steers traffic away from highway construction.

Then it processes the information and works out the best way to do its job.

But a robot doesn't think the way a person does. It can only do things that engineers and roboticists program into its computer "brain".

Tech Talk

PROGRAM: To give a set of instructions to a machine

ROBOTICIST: A person who builds robots

Researchers built the first robots about fifty years ago. But people had been thinking about mechanical "humans" for a long, long time.

850 BC	AD 1495	1961	1970
Ancient Greek poet Homer described bot-like creatures that did anything their masters asked.	Italian artist and scientist Leonardo da Vinci drew plans for a mechanical man in his notebooks.	The world's first robot went to work assembling cars at a General Motors plant in Ewing, New Jersey, USA.	Roboticists in Stanford, California, USA, built the first robot that could move and sense its surroundings.

Saturn

1977	1996	1999	2011
The Voyager 1 and 2 space probes were launched to study Saturn, Jupiter and their many moons.	Researchers at Honda introduced P2, the first human-like robot.	Sony developed AIBO, a robotic dog that could interact with people.	R2 was launched to the International Space Station, making it the first human-like robot in space.

Every robot is designed for a specific job. What the robot looks like will depend on the job it does. But no matter what a robot does, it has three kinds of parts – a computer, sensors and actuators.

A robot's computer is like a person's brain. It uses the instructions programmed by a roboticist to make decisions. The sensors are like a person's eyes, ears, nose and skin. They collect information about the robot's surroundings and send messages to the computer. A robot's actuators receive messages from the computer. They control the robot's movements, lights, speaking, and more.

Tech Talk

SENSOR: A robot part that detects light, temperature, pressure, sound or motion

ACTUATOR: A robot part that performs an action

Video camera to "see"

Microphone to "hear"

The Carnegie Science Center, USA, displays RoboThespian.

Sensors to "feel" heat, cold or pressure

weird but true

Some robotic sensors detect things people can't, like magnetic fields.

7 Cool Robots

Robots can do lots of interesting things. Which of these awesome robots would you like to have?

1

Each year, NAO (Now) bots compete in an international robot football match. Researchers make improvements after watching the robots play.

2

Inkha is a life-size robotic head that could greet people at a shop or doctor's office.

3

RoboLobster may one day search the ocean floor for mines and sunken ships.

4

RIBA was designed to lift patients from a bed or the floor.

5

HRP-4 is lean and light, and can stand on one leg. It also responds to voice commands.

6

In China, robotic waiters zip around restaurants delivering meals.

7

RoboTuna swims to explore deep ocean areas and coral reefs.

Go Bots!

All robots have movable parts, but only some can travel from place to place. That's because it's difficult and expensive to build bots that can travel far.

Robots that work in factories may not need to move very far. But when a bot has to get around, roboticists choose one of three systems – tracks, wheels or legs.

Tracks

Robots with tracks are rugged and reliable. They are perfect for moving across uneven ground, but they move slowly. Engineers design them to disarm bombs, fight fires and travel in space.

This robot disarms bombs for the US Marine Corps. It moves around on tracks to do its job.

track

track

A robot at a sewage treatment plant in France uses four wheels and solar energy.

Wheels

Robots with wheels are fast, but they may tip over on bumpy ground. Roboticists build them to mow lawns, guard prisons, patrol buildings at night and carry materials inside factories and hospitals.

Legs

Robots with legs can step over objects or climb up walls. They are perfect for cleaning up chemical spills or exploring uneven areas of the ocean floor.

This four-legged robot was designed to explore the site of a nuclear accident in Japan. It carries a smaller robot that fits into small spaces.

Nature Knows Best

Roboticists also study animals for ideas about how robots could move. Borrowing ideas from nature is called biomimetics.

These little ladybird robots move just like the insects they are named after.

Tech Talk

BIOMIMETICS: Copying the shape and movement of animals in a machine's design

This robot moves and climbs just like a gecko lizard. That makes it perfect for searching for injured people after tornadoes or earthquakes.

Animals are really good at moving around on this planet. They hop across rocky cliffs. They slither and scuttle over sand. They fly and swim and tunnel underground. Robots can also be made to move in many of the ways that animals move.

LS3 is being designed for the US Army to carry heavy packs for soldiers.

The LS3 robot has legs that work like a dog's. It can follow a person and move safely around trees and rocks. Engineers hope that one day the robot will follow spoken commands like a loyal dog.

A robot named Cyro, which is the size of a beach umbrella, moves through the water just like a jellyfish. The US Navy plans to use the bot to keep watch over coastal waters. Cyro could also make maps of the ocean floor and study sea life.

A thick layer of a squishy material called silicone gives Cyro a body that looks like a real jellyfish.

Imagine a robotic snake coming to life by remote control. As the robot wriggles from side to side like a python, its mechanical body slowly inches forward. There are tiny cameras all along the robot's body, so you can see what the robot snake sees.

A real tiger python

This snake could help with rescues in natural disasters. Snakes are the perfect shape to navigate through collapsed buildings after an earthquake. They can go where people can't.

Tech Talk

NAVIGATE: To locate a place and plan a path to get there

Robot snakes, called snakebots, can climb trees and swim, too.

Weird but true

Doctors use tiny snakebots during some operations because they can curve around body organs.

Robots at Work

Most robots do jobs that people can't do or don't want to do. If you can think of a job that is boring or dangerous, there is probably a robot that can do it.

Robots control some city trains at night, so human workers can get a good night's sleep. Factory robots arrange chocolates in boxes, spray-paint cars, build computers and perform many other jobs.

Car companies depend on robotic arms to do dozens of jobs. These factory robots are welding together metal parts.

Robots have no trouble working in blistering heat, freezing cold or places that smell bad. They can explore active volcanoes, visit distant planets and spend days tracking enemy soldiers in the desert.

This computer art shows the ACTUV robot ship that is designed to track enemy submarines for up to 90 days at sea.

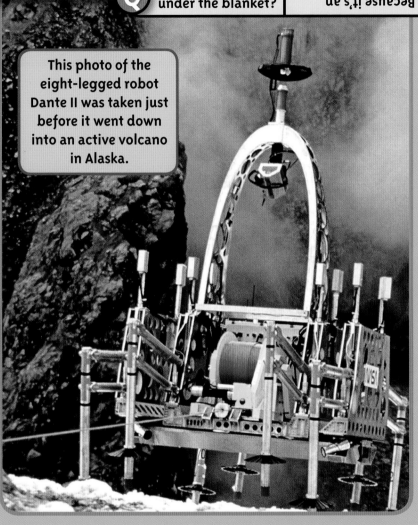

This photo of the eight-legged robot Dante II was taken just before it went down into an active volcano in Alaska.

Robots are useful workers because they don't take holidays or stop to eat lunch. All they need to do their job is power from an electricity supply.

Robots at Home

You don't need to push or turn this lawnmower. It senses when it has reached the edge of your lawn and turns itself.

Nobody likes mowing the lawn, so roboticists invented a bot to do the job. It senses an invisible fence, so it doesn't leave the garden.

In Tokyo, you can buy a piano-playing robot for roughly £32,000!

Nobody likes to do housework, either. So now there are robots that can vacuum your carpet. When a vacuum bot senses a wall, it backs up and rolls in a new direction.

There is also a robot alarm clock on wheels. If you don't get up, the bot jumps off your bedside table and rolls around your room. You have to get up to turn it off.

Robot alarm clock

Imagine having a robot that cleans your room. The El-E fetch bot can do just that. Point a laser at any object you want and the robot races across the room, picks it up and delivers it to you.

Roboticists hope that one day the El-E fetch bot will answer voice commands. For now, people use a laser pointer to give it directions.

Q Why was the robot upset?

A Because someone kept pushing its buttons!

Yurina can be controlled by a touch screen, a joystick or voice commands.

Researchers designed the El–E fetch bot to help people who have trouble getting around, but one day it could be in homes all over the world.

Roboticists are also hard at work on Yurina. It is designed to help people who are sick or disabled take a bath or move from a chair to a bed.

29

Pushing the Limits!

What did roboticist Kogoro Kurata have in mind when he set out to build the world's biggest bot? He just wanted to see if he could. Kurata is like a lot of roboticists. They try new things just to see if they're possible.

Computer artwork of a medical nanobot in the bloodstream

Other roboticists are working on bots so small they could swim through a person's blood. One day, these nanobots might be able to attack cancer cells or carry medicine to just one part of the body.

Tech Talk

NANOBOT: A robot so small you need a microscope to see it

Kurata's robot is the biggest robot ever made. You have to climb high to sit in the control seat of this four-metre-tall robot.

Almost Human

Researchers at Honda have been building robots that look and act like humans for more than 15 years. The latest version is called ASIMO. It can dance, balance on one leg, and even climb stairs. It can pick up objects, speak to people, and recognise faces and voices. Wow!

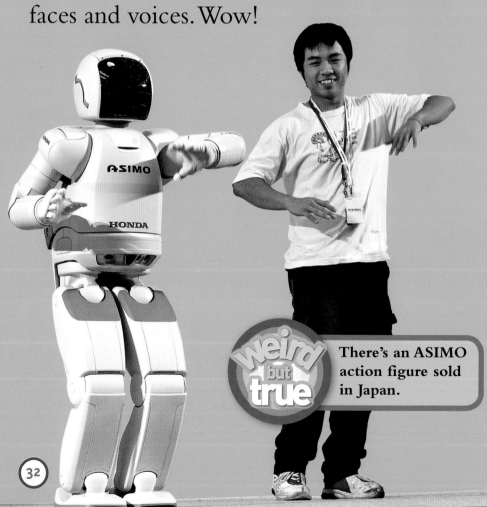

weird but true

There's an ASIMO action figure sold in Japan.

Schoolchildren in Tokyo, Japan, answer questions from their android teacher, Saya.

Androids are lifelike robots. Everything about them is artificial, but sometimes it's hard to tell they aren't real. Some androids seem to blink, breathe, twitch and talk just like a real person.

Tech Talk

ANDROID: A robot that looks or acts like a person

ARTIFICIAL: Made by humans

A roboticist named Cynthia Breazeal taught her robot Kismet about feelings. When she started, Kismet was just like a baby. She programmed it to like brightly coloured toys and people and to want to rest. She gave it 16 computers and many cameras – sensors for sight.

Roboticist Cynthia Breazeal works with Kismet. It reacts to what she does.

angry

Kismet can make different faces to show emotions.

disgusted

sleepy

Then she invited children and grown-ups to come and play with Kismet. When Kismet's cameras saw a happy, smiling face, Kismet learned to react in a very human way – by smiling back!

happy

Real Robots or Movie Magic?

Real robots can't move or speak as well as the robot characters you see in movies like *Star Wars* or *WALL-E*. What you see on the screen is the result of movie magic.

Can you name these robots from films? (Answers are on page 37.)

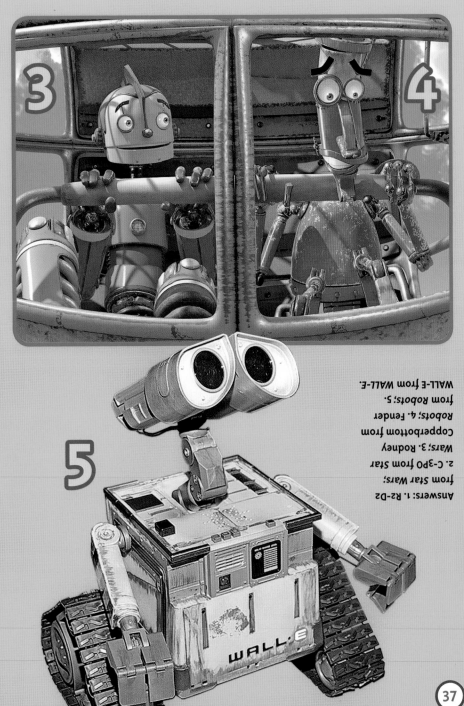

3

4

5

Answers: 1. R2-D2
from Star Wars;
2. C-3PO from Star
Wars; 3. Rodney
Copperbottom from
Robots; 4. Fender
from Robots; 5.
WALL-E from WALL-E.

WALL·E

Robots in Space

Robots can explore places that humans can't go. Humans have travelled to the moon, but robots have landed on Mars and they've collected information while circling Venus and Jupiter. Robots have also travelled to the edge of our solar system and even beyond it.

In 1977, scientists launched two Voyager spacecraft into space. These spacecraft have travelled more than 11 billion miles and are still sending information back to Earth.

An illustration of Voyager 1, a spacecraft built by NASA engineers to photograph and study Jupiter, Saturn and their moons

R2 can grasp handheld tools and lift up to 18 kilograms. It doesn't need to sleep or eat or go to the toilet like people do.

R2 has been aboard the International Space Station since 2011. The human–like robonaut uses camera sensors in its head to see. R2's computer is in its belly. One day, robonauts may work side by side with human astronauts.

Tech Talk

ROBONAUT: A robot astronaut

Two rover robots are exploring Mars. Opportunity has been cruising around the red planet since 2004. Curiosity landed in 2012.

Computer art of Opportunity

Computer art of Curiosity

Both bots are studying the planet's air, soil and rocks. Scientists are looking for signs of ancient life on Mars. They also want to know how much of the planet was once covered with water.

Armed and Ready

Curiosity's two-metre-long robotic arm is loaded with tools. Its wire brush clears away Martian dust. Its hammer drill pulls rock samples from below the surface.

Scientists designed Curiosity for a two-year mission, but they hope it will continue to send back information for much longer.

You Can Build Bots

Think you'd like to build a bot? You're not alone. Each year, more than 200,000 children between 9 and 16 years old join *FIRST*® LEGO® League (FLL®). They work on teams that research and solve a science question or problem. Then they build and program LEGO® robots to do a series of jobs.

After about ten weeks of planning, building and programming, many FLL® teams get together at big events where they can win awards and prizes.

Sound like fun? Let your parents and teachers know. They can help you start an FLL® team at your school.

Robots of the Future

It will be a long time before a household bot does all your cooking and cleaning. But in just a few years, a robot might drive you to school.

Right now several companies are developing robotic cars that drive themselves. Covered with sensors, robo-cars are safer and use less fuel than the cars we drive today.

What other amazing robo-inventions will soon be part of our lives? We'll just have to wait and see.

This robotic car is taking pictures and mapping streets in Brasilia, Brazil.

Glossary

ACTUATOR: A robot part that performs an action

BIOMIMETICS: Copying the shape and movement of animals in a machine's design

NANOBOT: A robot so small you need a microscope to see it

ROBONAUT: A robot astronaut

ROBOTICIST: A person who builds robots

ANDROID: A robot that looks or acts like a person

ARTIFICIAL: Made by humans

NAVIGATE: To locate a place and plan a path to get there

PROGRAM: To give a set of instructions to a machine

SENSOR: A robot part that detects light, temperature, pressure, sound or motion

Index

Illustrations are indicated by **boldface.**